The Whole Works

Careers in a Police Department

Author
Margaret Reuter

Photographer
Eric Oxendorf

℗
Childrens Press

Library of Congress Number: 77-8113

1 2 3 4 5 6 7 8 9 0 81 80 79 78 77

Printed in the United States of America.

Library of Congress Cataloging in Publication Data

Reuter, Margaret.
      Careers in a police department.

      (The Whole works)
      SUMMARY: An overview of careers in a police depart-
ment, emphasizing the diversity and interrelationship
of various jobs.
      1.   Police — Vocational guidance — Juvenile literature.
[1.   Police Vocational guidance.   2.   Vocational guid-
ance]   I.   Title.
HV7922.R48   363.2'023   77-8113
ISBN 0-8172-0956-5 lib. bdg.

We wish to thank G. L. Wieczorek, Youth Officer of
the Lake Forest, Illinois, Police Department for
his helpful suggestions.

Contents

1 The Whole Works

A little child is missing. A car skids on wet pavement. It crashes into a telephone pole. A man and woman come home. They find that someone has broken into their house. Help is needed quickly.

Call the POLICE DEPARTMENT.

POLICE OFFICERS are the people who keep our towns and cities safe. They protect people. They protect homes. When an accident happens, police rush to the scene. They know how to rescue people from dangerous places. They know how to get things under control.

Wherever people live there are laws. The laws are rules that tell us what we can do and what we cannot do. Each law is meant to make a community a safe place. A law may tell us how fast we can drive a car. It may tell us where we can cross a street safely. There are laws that protect us in another way. They tell people it is wrong to hurt someone. It is wrong to steal something from someone. It is wrong to spoil a park or a public building by damaging it.

The police department is the enforcer of laws. It sees that laws are obeyed. Police officers protect us by making sure we are following safety rules. They protect us by arresting people who break laws and commit crimes.

Every place where people live has a local police department. Even a very small town has a police officer, called a MARSHAL. The more people who live in an area, the more police officers are needed. Most towns have a police force large enough so that someone is on duty every hour, day or night.

Large cities have police departments that are separated into precincts. Each precinct has its own headquarters. Each precinct protects the people within its limits. A city police department also has special divisions for handling different kinds of problems.

The police departments of small towns and cities are not separated into divisions. Patrol officers are trained to answer every kind of emergency call.

Besides town and city police departments, there are also county, state, and federal police departments. Each of these departments protects a certain area.

Let's find out how a police department is organized. We'll learn what the police department leaders do. We'll see how patrol officers are trained to perform their many duties. We'll learn about the youth officer's work in the community. We'll take a look at detectives, the crime investigators of the police department. And we'll see what part the crime laboratory plays in solving crimes. We'll find out how important communications are to the police department.

Maybe you will find more than one career in the police department that you would like to follow. There are many from which to choose!

2 The Leaders

A police department is always organized by rank. That means that there is one person who is the top officer. Other officers work under the top officer. They carry out orders.

The CHIEF OF POLICE, sometimes called the chief inspector, is in command of the police force. The chief manages the schedule for all the people in the department. And decides what jobs are most important and how each job should be done.

The chief needs to know the community well. The chief finds out what problems there are. There may be a traffic safety problem. There may be vandalism. There may be robberies. The chief needs to know what the people in the community expect from the police department.

If a special event is going to occur, the chief plans for extra officers to be on duty. They handle crowds of people and direct traffic. The chief plans the best ways to handle unexpected events, such as a major storm or disaster.

The chief needs to know a great deal about the patrol officers in the department. Perhaps one understands a foreign language. Another is unusually good at controlling crowds of people. One is able to get along well with young people. Another likes to speak to adult groups. When a patrol officer

with a certain skill is needed, the chief chooses the best person for the job.

A police chief is like a business manager too. The chief knows the cost of items the department needs. The chief plans a budget. And decides whether more officers should be hired. And what new equipment is needed.

The chief directs the other police leaders. They are command officers. A command officer is one who has the right to make decisions and direct other police officers. The chief's first assistant is called a DEPUTY CHIEF. Then come CAPTAINS. A captain is an officer who commands a precinct in a city police department. The captain acts as the chief of a particular section of the city.

Next in rank are LIEUTENANTS and SERGEANTS. A lieutenant is an officer who is usually in charge of several squads of patrol officers all working on a certain shift. A sergeant is in charge of one squad of patrol officers.

PATROL OFFICERS are the working force of the police department. They do not have the power to command other police officers. Yet each patrol officer is a leader too. The patrol officer has to know how to direct people. The patrol officer makes decisions when no command officer is there to give orders.

All command officers — from sergeant to chief of police— began their careers as patrol officers. They learned to do their jobs through training and hard work. They proved that they could be trusted to do their jobs well. They used good judgment. Other police officers respected them.

Patrol officers who want to become command officers have to pass tests. The tests show which ones will make the best leaders.

3 Patrol Officers

What kind of person becomes a PATROL OFFICER? Someone who wants the community to be a safe place. Someone who wants to be sure laws are obeyed. Someone who cares about people and wants to help them.

There are jobs for men and for women in the police department. The people who apply for jobs must be alert and intelligent. They must have a record of being honest. The people who apply are given tests. Written tests, and tests that show they are strong and agile. They must be able to run, climb, jump, and move quickly and easily.

People are needed who will use good judgment and make decisions quickly and wisely. People are needed who are courteous and dignified, who will act in a way that causes people to respect them and want to obey them. Police officers need to be patient. They deal with people who are weak or frightened. Sometimes they deal with people who are angry or confused.

Especially in large city police departments, people are needed who understand foreign languages. When people do not speak English and need help from the police department, someone has to understand them. It is important to have a patrol officer who speaks their language.

A person chosen to become a patrol officer is called a CADET. Cadets go to classes in a police training school. They learn about the police department and how it operates. They learn about the laws they will enforce. They study and practice ways of controlling traffic. They learn how to investigate an accident. They learn how to patrol an area or zone. And they learn how to write reports and keep records.

Cadets learn many ways of helping people. Giving first aid. Settling arguments. Controlling crowds of people and keeping crowded places peaceful and safe. Rescuing people from dangerous places.

All cadets are taught how to defend themselves. They learn boxing and judo. They learn when to use a revolver and how to shoot accurately.

After a cadet is trained, he or she becomes a RECRUIT, or beginner, in the police department. At first the recruit is on probation. Probation is the time when recruits prove they are able to do the things they learned in police school. They show that they will become good patrol officers.

What do patrol officers do? They do whatever they can to prevent accidents and crimes. They get used to their "beat," the areas they patrol. They watch traffic patterns and buildings and empty lots. They observe places that are unsafe. They report conditions that could cause trouble. They warn drivers when they are speeding. And they make sure people walk across streets at places where it is safe.

Patrol officers protect property by inspecting stores and offices and checking locks. They watch homes when the owners are away.

If there is an accident and a person is hurt or a car is smashed, a patrol officer investigates. If there is a report of broken windows or slashed tires, a patrol officer finds out

what happened.

If a crime occurs, a patrol officer is the first to reach the scene. The officer looks for pieces of evidence, things that will show how the crime happened. The officer sees that the evidence gets safely to police headquarters. If the patrol officer sees someone commit a crime, he or she tries to catch and arrest that person.

Patrol officers never know what kind of call will come next. A dog bites a letter carrier. Someone smells gas and thinks there will be an explosion. A baby is ready to be born. The mother needs a ride to the hospital.

Patrol officers keep in touch with police headquarters. They are called by radio when someone needs help. After each call is answered, a report of what happened must be written. The reports become part of a record. The record helps police officers find ways to prevent accidents and crimes.

Do you know all the ways that patrol officers get around? Sometimes they just walk. Walking is a good way to patrol a place where there are many people and heavy traffic. But if someone needs help in a hurry, the officer needs wheels. Usually a patrol car is used, but sometimes it is a motorcycle, or even a bicycle. Sometimes patrol officers are mounted. They sit high in a saddle on a police horse. It is easier to observe what is going on in a crowd of people from up there.

There are patrols that use airplanes and helicopters. The officers can watch over a large area. They may follow a criminal's car. They let other officers on the ground know the car's location. They can keep the criminal from escaping. Helicopter patrols locate trouble spots and warn motorists of dangerous conditions. During rush hours they make radio announcements. They tell which routes are clear. They can direct emergency trucks to places where motorists have car problems.

In cities that have a waterfront, power boats are used by some patrol officers. Patrol officers can reach some places more easily from the water. And they can keep watch of waterfront areas in places where a car could not go. If there is a boat accident, they go to the rescue.

4 Traffic Officers

Patrol officers have to know how to control traffic. They watch to see that drivers follow safety rules. They answer emergency calls. They investigate accidents. They protect the safety of other motorists when an accident happens.

In large cities there are hundreds of miles of streets and highways to be patrolled. Cars and buses, motorcycles and bicycles, all kinds of trucks seem to fill the city streets. People must wait to cross. Everyone must take turns at intersections. Otherwise accidents would happen.

Traffic lights and safety rules prevent many accidents. But sometimes accidents do happen. Sometimes traffic is heavy and everything slows down. A TRAFFIC OFFICER comes to help.

A traffic officer directs the drivers and the people walking. The officer tells which ones to move. And points in the direction it is safe to go. When the officer moves his or her arms or holds one hand up like a stop sign, drivers know what is meant.

Someone asks the officer a question. "Where is the nearest gas station?" Or "How do I get to the airport from here?" The traffic officer answers the question.

And also keeps watching the traffic.

A traffic officer works outdoors even when the weather is bad. The officer "talks" with a whistle to get the drivers' attention and get them to follow commands. Some people don't want to wait their turn. The traffic officer makes sure they do. If one car moves too far into an intersection, it blocks cars moving across its path.

Traffic officers take charge when there is an accident on one of the city streets. An officer puts out flares, burning lights that warn other drivers to slow down. The officer directs traffic around the accident. If someone is hurt, traffic officers give first aid, or they radio for an ambulance. If there is a fire, they put it out themselves or they radio for the fire department to send help.

Sometimes a truck overturns. Things spill out onto the road. Traffic officers try to protect the things from being damaged or stolen. They call for tow trucks to move damaged cars or trucks. They make sure no pieces of glass or metal are left on the pavement.

Traffic officers try to find out what caused the accident and whose fault it was. They draw a diagram, a kind of map. It shows what direction each vehicle came from and where the crash happened. The traffic officers may arrest a driver if they are sure that driver caused the accident. Then they have to write a report.

Traffic officers stop drivers who are speeding or making turns that are against the rules. Sometimes they warn a driver. Sometimes they give the driver a ticket. They are trying to prevent accidents. They stop drivers to warn them of unsafe conditions. Like a flat tire. Or a broken headlight.

What does the flashing red light on a patrol car stopped on a highway mean? Usually a traffic officer is giving help to a motorist. Not a ticket.

5 The Youth Officer

A YOUTH OFFICER is a police officer who wants to help young people. Keeping boys and girls safe is one part of the youth officer's job. Keeping them from getting into trouble by breaking laws is another part.

A youth officer needs special ability and special training. A youth officer has college training. The youth officer knows what things cause problems for boys and girls.

The youth officer is also trained as every patrol officer is. The youth officer helps other police officers understand youth problems. And helps young people understand why police must enforce laws.

The youth officer talks to school classes. The officer tells the young people how to cross streets safely. What the rules are for bicycling. And how to avoid dangerous places.

The officer invites them to visit the police headquarters. The young people see how calls come in, how a patrol officer is sent to help. They see the rooms where police officers go to school themselves. Perhaps they see a firing range where officers practice shooting at a target.

The youth officer gets to know the young people in the town or precinct. The officer learns what kinds of activities young people have and where they spend their spare time.

The officer tries to spot problems before they become serious. The youth officer wants to prevent young people from breaking a law and getting into trouble.

Someone calls to report that a young person has been seen throwing rocks at street lights. The youth officer investigates. The officer finds out who was damaging the street lights. Then the officer calls the parents or goes to their house. The officer wants to work things out with the young person and the parents so that it won't happen again.

A shopkeeper calls to report that he caught a child stealing items from his store. The youth officer investigates. Again the officer talks with the child. The officer wants to make sure the child knows that what he or she did was wrong.

A youngster is missing from home. The youth officer tries to find out whether the child ran away, or is lost, or is in danger somewhere. The youth officer alerts other patrol officers. Questions the child's friends. And tries to learn anything that will help the police find the missing child.

Many people in the community help the youth officer. Parent-teacher groups, church groups, Scout troops, and service clubs all help. They plan worthwhile activities for boys and girls.

School counselors help. They understand young people too. They are in touch with boys and girls every day. They can let the youth officer know when someone has a serious problem and needs help.

Everyone wants his town to be a safe place for children. No one wants a child to get into trouble.

6 The Detectives

Some patrol officers are good at crime investigation. A person with this skill makes a good DETECTIVE. A detective is a police officer who solves crimes. The detective's job is to find out who did it. To get evidence that will prove what happened. To see that the person who broke a law is found and arrested.

Detectives have to be quick-witted. They must think well. Use their imagination. Have a good memory. And understand people. Detectives hope to get useful information by talking to people. They have to decide whether people are telling the truth.

Detectives do not wear uniforms. They want to be able to move about without being known as police officers. They do not have regular work hours. They have to work at times when they can find and talk with people. That is how they get information to help solve crimes.

A detective's job may sound exciting. But sometimes the work is dull and tiresome. Tracing one person may take a long time. When the person is found he or she may not have useful information after all. Then the detective must find another "lead," a clue that will help locate a witness. A witness is someone who saw the crime take place. Sometimes

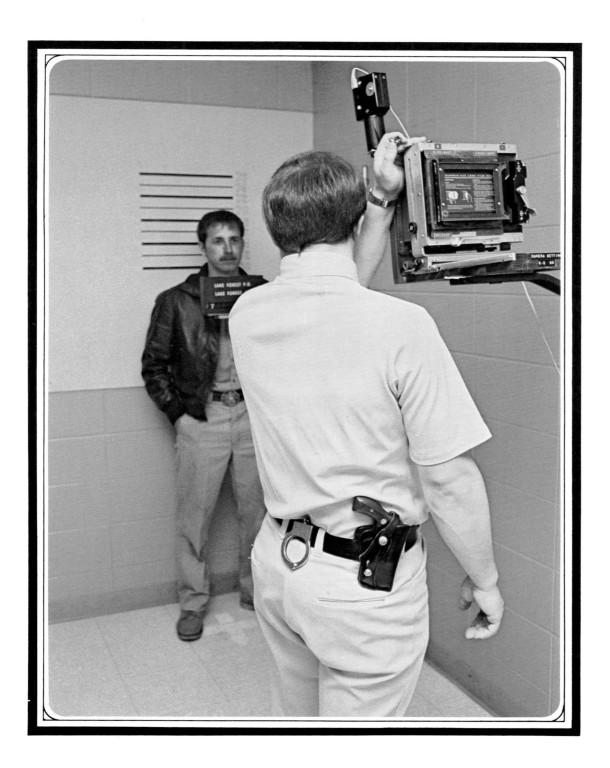

a detective has to search through files and records to check a single item. It might be very important.

The greatest number of crimes happen in large cities. City police departments have separate divisions of detectives. Each works on a special kind of crime. One division handles crimes in which a person is attacked. Another investigates crimes in which something is stolen. Another deals with crimes in which a person tries to cheat someone.

Some criminals commit the same kind of crime over and over. Some are muggers who surprise people by attacking them from behind and stealing money or jewelry. Some are bank robbers. Some know how to "crack" a safe, to open it and steal the money inside. Some are forgers who sign a false name to a check in order to get money. Such criminals get into certain habits and become known by the way they commit a crime. But detectives are specialists too. They learn the habits of different lawbreakers. They learn how to outsmart them. Sometimes they can guess who committed a crime from the way the criminal did it.

There are detective squads to investigate arson, gambling, drug abuse, and other kinds of "organized crime." The detectives try to find the person who committed the crime. But they also want to find the one who hired that person to do it.

Detectives cannot do their work alone. They need many helpers. The patrol officer who first goes to a crime scene helps by making a written report. A photographer helps with pictures of important evidence. A fingerprint expert helps. The expert makes copies of the marks left by people's fingers on anything touched at the crime scene. Then the expert compares these fingerprints with prints on file. The detective is given the name of the person who left the fingerprint. Sometimes an expert on guns helps. A gun expert can tell whether a certain weapon was used. Other laboratory workers help by analyzing bits of evidence to find clues.

7 Crime Laboratory Workers

CRIME LABORATORY WORKERS are scientists and technicians. Each scientist is an expert. Each knows a great deal about one special field. Each has a college education. And on-the-job training too. The scientists need experience in the crime lab. That is how they learn to use their special knowledge to help a detective solve a case. They learn to work quickly. Detectives need to get information as soon as possible.

Technicians help the scientists. They operate equipment in the lab. They use instruments to find out all about each piece of evidence. The technicians and lab assistants need special training too. Lab work must be done carefully, without mistakes.

Many lab workers are police officers who learned how to analyze evidence. Their experience helps them. They know it is important to be able to identify evidence.

What kinds of scientists work in crime laboratories? Chemists do. They can test any substance and tell exactly what it is made of. Experts on poisons do. They can tell if a poison caused a death and what kind of a poison it was.

Biologists work in crime labs. A biologist knows how to analyze a drop of fluid or a strand of hair. A biologist looks

through a microscope. It makes tiny particles appear large. What the biologist finds out may lead to the person who committed the crime. Or it may help to tell exactly who a dead person is.

Ballistics experts work in crime labs. A ballistics expert is a scientist who studies weapons and bullets. A ballistics expert knows how guns operate and how a bullet moves when a gun is fired. And can prove whether or not a bullet was fired from a certain weapon.

8 Communications Workers

A call for help for a traffic accident reaches police headquarters. The COMMUNICATIONS OFFICER radios a police patrol car. The car rushes to the scene of the accident. A witness remembers the license number of a hit-and-run driver. The patrol officer radios the number to headquarters.

At headquarters, a Teletype message is sent to a data bank where license numbers and owners' names are stored. Information is back in just a few seconds. The hit-and-run car was stolen. A description of the car is sent by radio to police patrolling the highway where the car drove away.

All this took place in a few minutes time. The system that makes this possible is called communications. Communications means getting a message from one place to another. By telephone. By radio. By Teletype. By computer.

If you must call the police and don't know the number, dial O. Tell the operator to call the police. Give the operator your address.

Perhaps you live where 911, the emergency police and fire department number, is used. Dial the numbers 9, 1, 1. Tell the communications officer why you need help. Give your address. Your call will be answered quickly.

Police departments use two-way radio. It works between

headquarters and a patrol car or walkie-talkie. It also works between one patrol car and another. A patrol officer can always get more help if it is needed.

Telephone and radio messages are tape-recorded at the communications center. A message that isn't clear can be played again. No messages are lost. Information cannot be forgotten.

The communications officer uses a teletypewriter to ask for information. The question goes to a data bank. A special machine called a computer finds the answer. It picks out the exact piece of information from the huge collection of facts stored in the data bank. It works faster than a person could speak. The answer appears on the teletypewriter as a typed message.

Data banks are used to store many things besides license numbers. They hold descriptions of stolen property and the names of missing persons. They contain records of crimes and criminals. And even of fingerprints.

Communications workers need special training. They must operate the machines that speed up messages. They must be quick. They must be careful not to make a mistake.

9 County, State, and Federal Police

You have been reading about the kinds of work people do in a city precinct or a town police department. Police officers work in other places too.

A police officer called a SHERIFF is in charge of all the places in a county where there is no local police department. The sheriff often has assistants called DEPUTY SHERIFFS. The deputies do the kind of jobs that police patrol officers do. They enforce the laws. They keep the county a safe and peaceful place.

A police officer called a TROOPER patrols state highways. The trooper sees that drivers obey the highway laws. The trooper answers emergency calls. Investigates accidents. And helps motorists. If someone has car trouble, the state trooper radios for a service truck. The trooper gives directions and answers questions. And tells people where to get off the highway to find a sightseeing place or a restaurant.

There are federal police departments too. They operate in the whole country. They enforce laws that we all must obey, no matter what town or what state we live in. One federal agency is in charge of protecting borders. It checks people who enter and leave the country. Other agencies enforce drug and alcohol laws. One agency enforces postal

service laws. The agency that is best known is the FBI, the Federal Bureau of Investigation.

FBI officers are called SPECIAL AGENTS. They are crime investigators. When a bank is robbed anywhere in the country, the FBI investigates. If a person is kidnaped, the FBI is called. Property that belongs to the government is protected by the FBI. If it is stolen or damaged, special agents are called.

The FBI has a fingerprint file. It has laboratories with special equipment. Whenever anything is sent to the lab to be analyzed, a report is made. Records are kept. There are so many fingerprints and so many records that data banks must be used to store all the information. Computers are able to find answers to all sorts of questions. A detective in a police department anywhere in the country can get help from the FBI records and files.

Each police department is formed to protect a certain area. But one department is always ready to help another one. They share information from their records. They help each other search for criminals. They exchange services. One department may offer the use of a firing range for target practice. Another may provide a laboratory so that nearby police departments can send evidence there to be analyzed.

10 Preparing to Serve

You can see that there are jobs in a police department for many kinds of workers.

Most police departments expect applicants to be high school graduates. But some jobs in police work take much more education than that. That is why a number of colleges have courses on law enforcement subjects. But just think of all the other courses a person could take that would help him to be a good patrol officer. An outstanding youth officer. A skillful detective. An expert in a crime laboratory.

Police department leaders know that more training helps police officers do their jobs better. That is why every department has programs for retraining officers. Patrol officers who want to be promoted to the rank of sergeant take special training in order to pass the tests. And there are courses that teach officers how to deal with special problems that arise in their community.

Police officers have to keep up with new laws. The policy of the police department itself may change. Community leaders may ask that certain laws be enforced more strictly.

A police officer is one employee who is expected to serve whenever needed. Even when not on duty. Police officers know that the work they do helps people in their community. They can feel proud of the way they serve.

Glossary

These words are explained the way they are used in this book.

ambulance—a car used to carry sick or hurt people to the hospital

analyzing—finding out what something is made of

arson—setting something on fire purposely

ballistics expert—a scientist who studies guns and bullets

biologist—a scientist who studies plants and animals and how they are made

cadet—a person training to become a patrol officer

captain—a police officer in charge of a precinct

chemist—a scientist who studies all kinds of substances

chief of police—the officer in charge of a police department

clue—something that suggests how to solve a crime

command officer—a police department leader

communications—a system of getting a message from one person to another

computer—a high-speed machine that finds answers

criminal—a person who does something against the law

crime—something that is against the law

crime laboratory—a place where scientists study evidence to help solve crimes

data bank—a place where many facts are stored

deputy chief—a person who assists the chief of police

detective—a police officer who investigates crimes

disaster—an event that causes loss or suffering to many people

drug abuse—using, buying, or selling drugs against the law

emergency—a serious event that requires fast action

evidence—anything that can be used to prove that a crime happened and explain how it happened

gambling—betting that is against the law

intersection—the place where two streets cross

investigation—finding out what happened and how

lieutenant—a police officer in charge of all the squads working on one shift

organized crime—a network of criminals with leaders who direct activities that are against the law

patrol officer—a police officer who is directed by command officers

police department—an agency that protects people and enforces laws

precinct—a division of a city police department

prevention—keeping something from happening

probation—a period when a patrol officer proves he is able to do his job

recruit—a beginning patrol officer

scientist—a person educated to be an expert in a certain kind of study

sergeant—a police officer in charge of a squad

sheriff—a police officer in charge of a county police department

special agent—a police officer in the Federal Bureau of Investigation

squad—a small group of patrol officers who train and work together

technician—a laboratory worker who uses special tools and instruments

Teletype—a way of sending messages quickly

traffic officer—a police officer who handles the movement of vehicles and investigates highway accidents

trooper—a police officer of a state police department

vehicle—a car, truck, or anything used to carry people or things on streets

youth officer—a police officer in charge of young people's problems and safety